What Happy Women

Know About Men And You Don't

By The Relationship DeCode™ Team

INTRODUCTION

You deserve so much better.

It's just that you don't believe you do.

That's about to change.

If you're like so many women – *especially when it comes to men and relationships* – you've probably had too many years of not being happy.

The men you've met have been less than impressive.

And...

The problems and baggage they bring has been more than desirable.

Yet you keep trying.

After many pauses, time outs, taking yourself out of the "looking for a guy" dating pool, you keep dipping your toes back into the water, all in the hopes that...

"This time will be different."

We have something to tell you...

It won't.

How do we know?

Because what you *say* you're looking for and what you *believe* you deserve, don't match.

Until it does, you'll keep getting what you've been getting.

Does that make you happy?

Good.

It shouldn't.

You deserve better.

You deserve to meet great men.

And they are out there looking for someone like you right now.

You might be asking…

"So if these great men are out there right now and they are looking for someone like me, how can I meet them?"

In life, we don't attract what we want.

We attract who we are.

The world knows who you are, by what you believe and that belief is translated into what you become and how you act.

One of the fastest ways to change your dating and relationship life, is to mirror what those who are already in happy relationships are doing.

They've already figured it out.

They've done the hard work for you.

So simply start doing what they're doing.

When it comes to men they'll date or the relationships they'll be in, these happy women have a list of things they look for in every man they're interested in.

Some of these are negotiable.

Others are not.

The choice is yours.

What you're about to read is their gift to you.

Think of it as...

Their Instruction Manual about what happy women really want in a guy and how men can give it to them.

Read it.

Soak it in.

Start believing you can have these things too.

And then watch how your belief begins to become a reality in your life.

Are you ready to uncover their secrets?

Here they are...

1

"Make Plans"

Ask enough to know what we like…
Then you take it from there.

2

"Listen To Us"

If we want answers or solutions... we'll ask.

3

"Stop Chasing Us So Much"

We like chasing too.

Remember... The more interested you are,
the less interested you need to act.

4

"Be More Confident"

The right kind of confidence (humble, respectful, kind, secure, and sure) can be a real turn on.

5

"Ask For Our Advice"

We have a kind of wisdom, insight
and understanding you don't.

6

"Have Dreams
And Goals"

Make them bigger than just paying your bills or buying
something you'll get tired of 3 months later.

7

"Be Fun"

The world is serious enough.

We like guys who can make us smile.

8

"Raise Your Standards"

You'll only attract quality women
if you're a quality person.

9

"We'll Test You"

You can only charm us with words for a short time.

We always watch your actions to know what you really believe and how you really feel.

10

"Put The Time In It"

Relationships, like anything in life, are as good as
the time you put into them.

Take the time for us… and we'll take the time for you.

11

"Do The Small Things"

Small acts of caring and kindness are much more desirable to us than buying us big expensive things to make up for your neglect.

12

"Know Yourself"

If you don't know what you want, then how do you expect us to help you get it?

13

"Ask For What You Want"

We're not mind-readers.

Don't assume anything. Be kind. Be thoughtful.
Be caring. And don't be shy to ask.

14

"Surprise Us"

Doing the same things over and over
(unless we "really" enjoy them) is one of
the fastest ways to put out the romance fire,
and for us to lose interest in
those things and in you.

15

"Honor Your Word"

Don't make promises you can't keep.
Once you lose our trust… you've lost us.

16

"We Love Momma's Boys"

If you've got a good mom, that is.

A great relationship with a great mom is
one of life's blessed gifts.

The smartest women look for that.

Knowing how to treat a woman begins
with knowing how to treat your mom – a woman you love with
honor and respect.

And if you know how to do it for your mom, there's a good
chance you'll know how to do it with us.

17

"Don't Put Us On A Pedestal"

We don't want it. We don't need it.
And we don't ask for it.

Love us. Respect us. Care for us. And you're there.

18

"Accept Our Good Friends"

We'll do the same for you.

They were our friends before we met you.
And chances are they'll still be our friends, if the time
ever comes, that you're no longer in our life.

19

"Don't Be So Shy And Afraid"

Even the most beautiful among us,
rarely get approached or asked out because guys think
we're too pretty and out of their league.

We're not.

Come talk to us.

20

"We Know When You're Talking Bull***t"

Saying words you think we want to hear never works...
for long. Get smart and don't even start.

21

"Follow Your Dreams"

And invite us to enjoy the ride
with you on the journey.

If you're the right one for us,
we'll be thrilled and excited to go along
with you and inspire you to make it happen.
And you'll love to do the same for us.

22

"Don't Be Afraid To Change"

If you keep doing what you're doing,
your life will be the same 3 years from now.

Does knowing that make you happy?

23

"Talking Is Sharing And Listening Is Caring"

You learn very little by talking so much about or just the things that interest YOU.

Look in the mirror.
You've got two ears and one mouth.

Listen twice as much as you talk.

24

"We've Got Our Own Money"

You've got yours.

If we get together, we'll figure out the best way
to spend and save it.

And we could care less who makes the most money.

There. We said it.

25

"Don't Even Try...
To Change Us"

We're not going to change. Never. Ever.
And the right woman will not ask you to either.

26

"We Are More Than Our Career"

And so are you.

Let's stop talking about them so much.

Let's also agree... to stop chasing after "worldly success" and other people's approval.

We're good enough just who we are.

27

"Love Us When We're Muddy"

The world can be a messy place.
People are not always the most thoughtful and kind.

We're going to have good days and days that just suck.

Love us and want to be with us during both, and you'll have
one of the best friends you will ever know.

28

"We Are Not Just These 3 Things"

It's been said, that to some men,
a woman will be a mistress in young age.
A best friend in middle age.
And a nurse to them in old age.

We like being your best friend the best.
And we like it when you are ours too.

29

"Arrive Happy"

Come to us happy and when you're
in a good place in your life.
The right one of us will meet you there.

We didn't sign up for being the people who fill
the missing pieces in your life.

We'll never be able to do that for you.
Nor do we want to.

Let's "add" to the happy people
who we already are.

"Have A Big Plan"

If you don't know where you're going,
how are you ever going to get there?

We may often ask you,
'What are your plans for your life?'

If you keep answering, 'I don't know',
then don't be surprised, if the day comes,
when we no longer ask you that question.

If you have potential.
If you have big plans and dreams.
If you are *trying* to be better and have a better life.
We will know it.

And we will be there to help you and cheer you on.

Do the same for us.

Think BIG. Dream BIG. Expect BIG.

Just think of what we can accomplish if we do it together.

31

"Give Us Plenty Of Time And Space"

When it's time to see and talk to you again,
we know who you are.
And we know how and where
to find you.

"Bring A Carry-On Bag"

We've all got baggage from the past.

That's just the way it is. It's all good. Bless it.

Thank all the people who were in your past.
We wouldn't be here with each other right now,
if we were still with them.

The past and the people in it helped us become who we are.

If you're looking for a great relationship,
here's a word to the wise...

"If you're bringing baggage to a new relationship,
just make sure it's a small carry-on."

And if we ever want to know what's inside that small
carry-on... we'll be the ones who'll ask.

33

———

"We Don't Need Needy"

Few things turn us off faster than a guy
who acts "clingy" and "needy."

We're not into guys who expect and look to us
to give them things they're missing in their life.
You've got a great life. Figure it out.
Give yourself what you need and we'll do the same
and all of us will be happier.

34

"Sighs Matters"

As in…
Doing the little things that take our breath away.

Like…
Asking how you can make our day better…

Surprising us with kind gestures…

Just "listening" for as long as we want to talk…

And doing the unexpected things
without us having to ask.

You're smart. You're wise. You're brilliant.
You're amazing.

It doesn't have to be every day.
Just show us from time-to-time,
why we made the best choice choosing you
and we'll do the same.

See… that was easy.

35

"Know What You Want
And Let It In"

Don't tell others you want to find
love and then not open the door when
love comes knocking.

We've all been hurt and disappointed.
Get over it. And if you can't or won't,
then we'll quickly get over you.

36

"Leave Your Past Behind You"

That includes relationships.
And we don't care to hear the details.

All we want to know is... "Did you learn something from it?"
and "Did it help make you a better person?"

Bless your past and all who were in it. We have.

Now come join us.

"Be Who You Really Are"

You fool no one but yourself.

We have ways of finding out the truth
about you very quickly.

38

"Be Well Rounded"

Be well versed in things of mind, spirit and body.

We love good conversations about
a lot of different things.

If you can hold our attention and talk freely,
openly and in-depth about them, then we'll love having
the chance to talk, to hold, and to be with you.

39

"Be Kind And Considerate"

Not only of us, but of others…
especially those less fortunate than you.

One of the fastest ways we know if we want to be
with you, is by how you treat others.

Be generous with your praise, gratitude,
and with the giving of your money to others,
and we'll be generous with our time
and commitment for you.

40

"Talk To Us About Something Other Than Our Looks"

There's already too much pressure
on women to look good.

Looks and other things change. Who we are doesn't.

We're smart, wise, and we can talk about anything and
everything. And most importantly, we want to.

So let's do.

41

"Behind Great Men Are Great Women. And Likewise"

A relationship with the *right woman*
is one of the most important and life-changing
decisions you will ever make.

Choose wisely.

The smartest, wisest and happiest of us still do.

42

"Grow In Love With The Right One"

The key to happiness in life,
relationships and love is, not to be in a relationship
with someone you can live with.

That's too easy and too common.

The key is...

You want to be with the one you
don't want to live without.

43

"Looks And Physical Beauty Come And Go"

Learn this lesson: Stop chasing women for their looks.

Outward appearance may first attract you,
but it's her essence, spirit, kindness, sense of humor,
compassion, caring, personality and soul
that will keep you.

44

"Always Remember: Someone Got Tired Of Someone"

Even the most physically beautiful people were once in relationships that didn't last.

When a relationship is ready to be over, it's going to be over.

Learn that lesson and consider yourself very wise.

45

"Great Relationships Don't Come With Owner's Manuals"

Few of us were ever taught how to find, be in, and have a great relationship.

Most of us learn by lots of trial and error.

Keep thinking of ways to make yourself
and a relationship better. And we will too.
We think all of us will be happy
with what happens.

46

"Look Ahead 20 Years To See What You Might Expect"

It's been said...

"If you want a preview of what the person you want to be in a relationship with may be like in 20 years, take a look at their mom and dad."

We think there's some truth in that.

The acorn doesn't fall too far from the tree.

Yes, people *can* always change.

Yet, let's be real here, shall we?

Human nature *is*...well, human nature.

We're just sayin'.

47

"We Remember Everything

That thing you forgot you said 8 months ago…
yeah, we remember it.

We remember everything.
So don't even try to fool us.

Be yourself. Speak your mind. Be truthful. Be honest.
Be loving. Be courteous, kind, caring and considerate.
Be respectful. And come at it all from
a good place, and all will be good.

48

"Take Good Care Of Yourself"

It's so easy to do.

Keep your hair and body clean.
Trim your fingernails and toe nails.
Trim your nose and ear hair. Brush your teeth and floss.
Make your bed. Wash and change your sheets.
Wash your clothes. Pick up after yourself.
Be organized. Exercise.

Simple. Powerful.

And we will notice it... and YOU.

49

"Looks Are Overrated"

The hotties and hunks attract the people
who simply haven't had enough experience with those
kinds of people to know any better.

The smartest of us value trust, commitment, honor, humor,
honesty, respect, courtesy, kindness and love.

If you've got those, then don't worry so much
about looks and the rest.

50

"If You Want To Be A Player, Do It In Sports"

We can spot you quickly and easily.
We know your number and we know your game.
So don't even try to fool us.

51

"Good Simple Formula To Remember:

Uncut + Unkept + Unclean = Us Uninterested In You"

Just so you know how important this is to us…

Uncut + Unkept + Unclean = Us Uninterested In You"

52

"Know 'The Car Test'"

And it's not what kind of car you drive.

"The Car Test" is looking inside of your car
to see how you really live.

A person's car is like their second home.
They spend lots of time in them.

If your car is cluttered and messy, there's a good chance
you're cluttered and messy too.

53

"The Big Turn On: Humble Confidence"

If you've got it. If you show it.
If you live it. And it's genuinely who you are.
Then there's a good chance you will have us
interested in getting to know YOU.

54

"Just Listen"

If we want answers or solutions, we'll ask.

It's THAT simple.

55

"Be Generous"

With your kindness. Courtesy. Happiness.
Inspiration. Praise. Compliments. Caring. Gratitude. Humor.
Good deeds. With your tips and charity to and for other people.

What you give out, comes back to you
multiplied many times over.

We like that.

"Wise Up. Grow Your Mind. Stupid And Unhappy Can Last Forever"

Grow your thinking.
Grow what you can conceive and believe is possible for you.

Then make it bigger and greater.

We admire boldness, initiative and a take charge
"I can do it" attitude.

We admire a belief that knows
what it wants… and is determined to not quit until
you get it… or something better.

57

"Be Happy, Grateful And Thankful"

The world is full of pissed off and unhappy people.
Don't be one of them.

Just having the gift of this amazing, blessed day
is enough for *anyone* to be thrilled about.

We are.

How about YOU?

58

"It's Easy To Find A Woman"

The most important thing is...
"Find the woman you don't want to live without."

You'd be very wise to remember that.

If you get no other advice from us and only remember this, your life will be changed positively, wonderfully, and amazingly.

59

"The Right Woman Will Find Time For You"

If a woman keeps making excuses or putting off making time for you, she's not interested.

With the right relationship, you *want* to make time for each other. And you *do*.

That feeling will come easily and naturally, without any coercion, manipulation, guilt or games.

60

"Enjoy The Moment. That's All We've Got"

With the right person,
it's doubly good.

With the wrong person,
it's doubly miserable.

Choose carefully. Choose slowly. Choose wisely.

If you understand the importance of this, then count
yourself as one of the wisest people on this earth.

Go to RelationshipDecode.com
for more books, audios, videos and products from
the Relationship Decode™ Team.